The Slaughterhouse of Dreams

THE SLAUGHTERHOUSE OF DREAMS

KASALA FOR MY KAKU

Fiston Mwanza Mujila

Translated from the French by

J. Bret Maney

DEEP VELLUM
DALLAS, TEXAS

Deep Vellum Publishing
3000 Commerce Street, Dallas, Texas 75226
deepvellum.org · @deepvellum

Deep Vellum is a 501c3 nonprofit literary arts organization founded in 2013 with the mission to bring the world into conversation through literature.

Originally published in French as Kasala pour mon Kaku et autres poèmes. by Maison de la poésie d'Amay / l'Arbre à paroles, Amay, Belgium, 2021

Published by agreement with Pontas Literary & Film Agency.

First English edition, 2025

Support for this publication has been provided in part by grants from the Texas Commission on the Arts, the City of Dallas Office of Arts and Culture, and the Addy Foundation.

Library of Congress Cataloging-in-Publication Data

Names: Mwanza Mujila, Fiston, 1981- author | Maney, J. Bret translator
Title: The slaughterhouse of dreams / Fiston Mwanza Mujila ; translated from the French by J. Bret Maney.
Other titles: Kasala pour mon Kaku et autres poèmes. English
Description: First English edition. | Dallas, Texas : Deep Vellum, 2025. | "Originally published in French as Kasala pour mon Kaku et autres poèmes by Maison de la poésie d'Amay / l'Arbre à paroles, Amay, Belgium, 2021"--Title page verso.
Identifiers: LCCN 2025027153 (print) | LCCN 2025027154 (ebook) | ISBN 9781646054114 paperback | ISBN 9781646054121 ebook
Subjects: LCSH: Mwanza Mujila, Fiston, 1981---Translations into English | LCGFT: Poetry
Classification: LCC PQ3989.3.M94 K3713 2025 (print) | LCC PQ3989.3.M94 (ebook) | DDC 841/.92--dc23/eng/20250626
LC record available at https://lccn.loc.gov/2025027153
LC ebook record available at https://lccn.loc.gov/2025027154

Cover photo by Sammy Baloji
Exterior design by Justin Childress
Interior layout and typesetting by David Wojciechowski

PRINTED IN THE UNITED STATES OF AMERICA

Contents

List of Photographs

kasàlà: a Luba praise song or poem

KASALA FOR MYSELF 1

I decided to be happy
to dance the rumba till I'm beat
to take back all my names, shards of the past
to remain the child of the mine and railroad
family memory coupling with the locomotive
exile in the bud, loneliness without end

I decided to be insolent, and unseemly
to spit in the soup of those who defang life
to piss on their supposed good faith
to snicker in insolence
and repent, later, to the Elder Spirit
for how long can they really last?
already, they have made this country a grave

I decided to turn out dreams
as vast, as colorful, as high-flying
as hope
sumptuous dreams
slobbering like tropical rain
alone expectorating the curse
upsetting all in its wake
furious, eternal, worthy of the flood
though this time they won't march into the Ark
the male and the female
the pair of all clean beasts

I decided to remain the child of Zaire
to fashion derby cars from tin cans
and kites from bags
attaching a long string
and running through the sunshine, running and running
until the kite leaped heavenward . . .
when the raffia string snapped

the zigzagging kite was lost in the sky
and regret was all we had

I decided to dream again
not of walking on the moon or
inventing an umpteenth WMD
but of opening a sort of magical bar
where I'd sell not drunkenness, or binges
but hope

I decided to be my fate's own one-man band
myself on drums: KENNY CLARKE
myself on trumpet: MASEKELA
myself on piano: TAPSCOTT
myself on double bass: MINGUS
myself on sax: SANDERS
in the background MAKEBA's voice
to groove from dawn to dawn
and hum for my mother (MA'NANGA) and the stars
Indépendance cha-cha

KASALA FOR MYSELF 2

Mwanza Mbala
Mwanza Nkangi
male serpent
female serpent
hurled from high heaven
for nonchalance lined with insolence
I've become by purest chance
Mwanza Nkongolo, the Rainbow
who seeks the sky in a middle ground
who halts the rain and its mishandling

KASALA FOR MY KAKU 1

my great-grandfather, Kaku, as we affectionately knew him
had lived forever
he was 105, 120, 134, 142, 157, 169, 186, 192
years old
maybe even two centuries in age
my Kaku was such an antique he'd long ago stopped notching the years
he could no longer even guess in which century he was born

my Kaku was as old as the sun
my Kaku was as old as the flood
my Kaku, yes, my Kaku, was as old as the Zambezi River
my Kaku was as old as the Mississippi
my Kaku was as old as the Danube
my Kaku was as old as the Lubumbashi–Ilebo Railroad
my Kaku was as old as New Guinea *(x 5)*

more than once, my Kaku had wanted to die
but death had boycotted his door
every morning, on the veranda, facing the sun
we settled him into his rocking chair
we fed him at noon
at nightfall, Kaku was still working his jaws
then we put him to bed

the body, his body, Kaku's body
no longer responded
old age had sapped his mobility
leaving only his voice and memory unscathed
Kaku chattered without stint
Kaku recounted his early childhood in Dimbelenge
Kaku retold his turbulent youth
Kaku went on and on about his life
in the mines of Bakwanga and Katanga
Kaku, with his legendary verve, retraced the family exodus

reeled off the genealogy of Mwanza wa Mwanza
summoned up memories of Zaire
expatiated on the first war in Shaba
evoked Lumumba, the massacre of the Katekelayi diggers
the secret agents of the Second Republic . . .

nestled in his rocking chair
an oceanic beard lapping at his chin
my Kaku turned prophet
augured Republics to come
incandescent stars, railroads connecting all points of the nation
cities drunk on light, populations dumbfounded
with the same verve, the same joy, the same
spittle, my Kaku talked, my Kaku talked, my Kaku talked . . .

(laughter)

what homesickness, what melancholy, what solitude
what anguish
we, the centipedes, taking up arms against a wretched life
while Kaku, up above
between heaven and earth
chuckles at us
Kaku
                    Kaku
                                        Kaku
          Kaku
Kaku

KASALA FOR MY KAKU 2

Mvidi Mukulu, the Elder Spirit, condemned my Kaku
to an absurdly long life
Kaku grew old, declined
but did not perish
he bragged of his birth in 1667, 1756, or 1786
one time, he even winked out for half an hour
then was raised from the dead as if nothing had occurred

protester of the first rain, fine looking fellow
from the peak of his three centuries of age
my Kaku had the quick blood of a lad

KASALA FOR SAYAKA

before meeting you
Japan and its blossoms
hardly moved me
not unlike math, chemistry, or astrology
a secret known only to the initiated
like a dead language or a randy volcano
but ever since that day
they bloom in me like poetry
Rotterdam (with or without wheels) is a city of miracles

SELF-PORTRAIT 1

look at my body
saggy
sinister
feculent
harebrained
pockmarked
coughed up by the mangrove
slimy, lanky, liquescent
hair sprouting from my mouth
it's my body alright
this body

BEFORE THE BANISHMENT

the Animals did not become Animals
as we know them today
until cast out of high heaven
in the beginning, the Animals
and Bende, the First Human
and all Things dwelt elsewhere
no animal swished its tail
no animal marched on four legs
no animal chewed cud or meat
all used the Word
were equivocal creatures
half human, half animal
and stamped with the seal of eternity
because born under the same stars
as the Great Spirits
molded by the very hands
of Foremother Tshiame

when I was a boy
I halted the rain
with a wild frond
I wove myself
while humming a tune
about a great river
and twins—
born half a year apart—
but bringing the sun to heel
that, I never dreamed of
you'd have to be six sheets to the wind
sprint stark naked through the streets
to stop it in its tracks
on its casual path of fire

GENESIS

we will make children
wherever the grass grows
children in such numbers
they will die of thirst
like a parched lawn
the machine will spin forever
rolling out children day and night
until half the universe clots
with their squealing and cries

IDEAL GEOGRAPHY OF THE ZAIRE RIVER

(dream route: from Katanga to the ocean, detour to Uíge and Ondjiva in Angola, return to Zaire and hasty departure to Bobo Dioulaso)

the river travels across thousands of kilometers
and offs itself into the ocean—
well done!
but I see only stupidity in this show

we ply you with food and wine
give you pet names, shake our hips
and applaud you with both hands
but you, to everyone's shock
(since your frantic descent into the ocean is no less)
instead of doubling back
or entering Angola, leaving, and recrossing
the country, as is your wont, towards Douala or KwaZulu-Natal
defenestrate yourself into the ocean
without even paying your bills or the rent
it's enough to make us Zairians dizzy

MINER'S SONG 2

when we pass away our moms
will bear children more precious than us
when they pass away
from a cavity or a cave-in
our moms will have children
rougher, more unkempt than us
when they pass away our moms
will bear children, thousands more children
to take up the work
our moms will have children
our moms will have children
more children to feed the mine

JOY

in his bar
my grandfather holds court at the counter
he is as happy as the sun

SELF-PORTRAIT 2

Foremother Tshiame!
tell me if the voice who speaks within
is really I
Mwanza wa Mwanza
or my grandmother

bah, I've always been my grandmother
how could I not be
with my elongated Mangbetu skull?
there's no need to chug djudju juice
or skim the night skies of Ngandajika or huff glue—
CIRCULATE!
I *am* Julienne Mwa Mwanza

we asked the Elder Spirit
to punish us, to drive us to suicide, to kill us in our sleep
to give us epilepsy, or even smallpox
but he made no reply

we took his silence
for a ruse
we begged him
(without mincing words)
to use tear gas or drop an atomic bomb
to plunge us in the rapids
and abandon us in the wake
and, while at it, to forsake
our skeletons
our pates and skulls
to leave them at the mercy of mermaids
and marine animals
but he made no answer

two months later
he rolled out the heavy artillery
we were caught off-guard
each resting in his own spot
slack-jawed
suddenly wetting our pants
then the most fearful among us, the born cowards, squealers, errand boys and girls, deposed pimps, Sunday hookers, miners, and hawkers of second-hand shoes
started waving our arms
and legs, vanquished
crying out, jabbering in anonymous tongues
empty flatteries and other nonsense
we are so sorry

Mvidi Mukulu wa Tshiame
Foremother Tshiame
I earned the highest marks in inanities
I sent forth lightning bolts for trifling matters
I danced in my birthday suit under the midday sun
I called Mikombo wa Kalewa
every nasty name I know
now my head hurts
and I have no twin sister
to blame somebody else
no sinecure to which I can aspire
must I retreat to my own country
ask Auntie Ntumba Annie
to scrub me clean from head to toe
or go digging up diamonds with Tshimbalanga
the second youngest of my uncles

I want to write a poem
the same way I'd like to trade heads
rebuke the stars
balance a boat on my brainpan
and search the streets of St. Louis
for Mr. Akinmusire and his trumpet—
trim my goatee with a hacksaw
micturate in the trees
dance a jig
slurp a river dry
set the sun on fire
raise a cathedral
and sell stone fruits within

WALTZ FOR LUMUMBA

after the song of the same name

Lumumba eats an apple
Lumumba dances salsa
Lumumba goes skiing
Lumumba in astronaut garb
Lumumba playing sax
Lumumba drives his car
Lumumba at his birthday party
Lumumba loves reggae
Lumumba nurses his beer
Lumumba in suit and tie
Lumumba at the airport
Lumumba laughs as never before
Lumumba sporting an afro
Lumumba and his dreads
Lumumba punk!
rock 'n' roll
Lumumba in Accra
Lumumba in Brussels
Lumumba gives his speech
Lumumba gets locked up
Lumumba dies
Lumumba expands
Lumumba is on TV
Lumumba is on the radio
Lumumba is in Uíge
Lumumba is in Moscow
Lumumba crosses the river
Lumumba takes the metro
Lumumba is in the bush
Lumumba, Lumumba, Lumumba, Lumumba
Lumumba, Lumumba, Lumumba, Lumumba
Lumumba, Lumumba

FAMILY TREE

a man and a woman
meet at stream's edge
sparks fly
they go back to the village
arm-in-arm
they fuck all night long
the man goes off to find something to drink
the woman goes about her business
they meet again that night
for another round of the beast with two backs
carried on until dawn
months go by
the seasons change
they have many children
each of these children
finds a boy or a girl of their own
they make the beast with two backs
and their progeny multiplies
one of the boys meets a girl
they have a boy
this boy and another girl have a girl
this girl and another boy have a boy
this boy and another girl have a girl
this girl and another boy have a boy
this boy meets a girl, they have a girl
this girl and a boy have a boy
this boy and a girl have a boy
the births go on, the babies
grow up, they move to the center of the country
or to Tanzania or Uíge, in Angola
at the whim of the trains
among those who return
a girl meets a boy
later on, they have a girl

this girl and a boy have a girl
this girl and another boy have twins
one of the twins dies young
his brother, as if to avenge him
has three sets of twins of his own
who scatter across the country
one is a boy who meets a girl
these two young people have a boy
the boy and a girl have a girl
the girl and a boy have children of their own
one is named Mwanza Mujila Bisonsa
he's not the type to stay in one place
he discovers he has a gift for trade
he travels to a faraway district called Bukama
he buys fish and meat that he returns to resell in his village
one fine morning, he meets a young woman named Mpinda
they have several children
including Mwamba Kabuya
Mwamba Kabuya meets Odia Julienne
who becomes known, later on
(owing, no doubt, to her formal manner)
as Julienne Mwa Mwanza
they have several children
including Mwanza Mujila
Mwanza Mujila meets Nanga Musadi
or perhaps Nanga Musadi meets Mwanza Mujila
(it depends who you ask)
they have eight children
including Mwanza Mujila Fiston
better put, Mwanza wa Mwanza Mujila—
first names not being worth this paper they're printed on

TSHILUBA LESSON

for Kalaf Epalanga

sun = diba
rain = nvula
moon = mutotu
sky = diulu
earth = buloba
tree = mutshi
food = biakudia
village = musoku
house = nzubu
speech = diyi
heart = moyi
river = musulu
uncle = tatu mwakunyi
life = nsombelu
exile = tshimwanyi
train = kawulu
goat = mbuji
birth = diledibwa
voyage = luendu
song = musambu
rainbow = Mwanza Nkongolo

AMNESIA

for Noralyne Moranus

we talk and write
in languages brought by train and boat
imported, manufactured languages
unknown to our ancestors
Julienne Mwa Mwanza, my grandmother
did she hum in Flemish?
Kaku, my great-grandfather, did he grouse in French?
closer to our own time, the second youngest of my uncles, Tshimbalanga
lost to the diamond mines, did he gamble his stones in German?

when our Elders declared
(in plain speech)
that Mvidi Mukulu made the dry season, the rain, the village, the banana trees
and humans long after the creation of the animals
the same animals that once roared with laughter
walked upright, and talked with ease—
but in what language?
was it Spanish they spoke?

PROCREATION'S MANY LITTLE SECRETS

losing your wits?
certainly not!
according to the defunct, the elders, and the ancestors—
those born before the full moon
those on the receiving end of revelations
without falling into the bottle
(or suffering the insomnia of these last days)—
things are expressed in lush language
they all possess an age, a mouth, and a gender

rain = feminine
stones = masculine
grass = feminine
fire = masculine
water = feminine
darkness = masculine
stars = feminine
birds = masculine
aquatic animals = feminine
land animals = masculine
men (during the rainy season) = feminine
the rainbow = feminine and masculine
because it binds two serpents
the female and the male

this feeling of being born
in Sarajevo every time I think of Europe
is it chance or a two-cent dream?

ANNA

Netrebko, we thirst for your voice
we can't sleep, we can't eat
we don't even shower
if you sing us a song
we will give you a piece of the river
baskets of vegetables and fruits

TSHILUBA LESSON 2

one = umua
two = ibidi
three = isatu
four = inayi
five = itanu
six = isambombo
seven = muanda mutekete
eight = muanda mukulu
nine = tshitema

MY LOVES

I keep three pets
the Zambezi, the Danube, the River Zaire

NORWICH

its many churches from the Middle Ages
its endless row of pubs
where you gulp wine, beer, love, water, hope
its narrow streets paved with poetry
its market stalls with their flamboyant roofs
its castle overhanging the town
and its almost tropical climate
the rain making its presence felt at will
a salad or noodle bowl at Frank's Bar
to sit alone and mend your silence
or wend your way up Dereham Road
on a borrowed bicycle
all this brings to my anguish
ten thousand years of sunlight

DELINQUENT JOY

conscience—
if the Earth boycotts us much longer
if the Earth breaks our little toes
if the Earth sells us for peanuts
if the Earth stops us from getting blitzed on bissap
if the Earth relieves herself on our heads
we will make a new planet
in a fit of pique, bad faith, and despair
we will give everything new names
we will replace the stars with LEDs
and auction off our rivers, rain, and typhoid fever

compassion—
Mvidi Mukulu, the Elder Spirit
watches us, the loafers and merrymakers, from his throne
we are dazed by joints and cheap beer
tanked up, cutting loose on the dancefloor
he loses his patience but smiles wanly
threatens us with fire and the flood
dusts off some vial of an epidemic spread by flies
or schedules an earthquake
only to relent at the last second

tenderness—
exuding the same scent of jasmine
kneaded from the same flesh
we force-feed the same loud dreams:
alcohol, time, saudade
and to think that the color of my skin makes commerce with the night
I hail from Central Africa, you, from a Europe of windswept rain and mild winters
between us, the desert, but what does it matter, I am you, you are me
we are angels boycotting the sky
angels who must go on without God

angels with no-fixed-address
indescribable shards
braving the sun and the end of the world

courage—
for years, we have dreamed of the sun
not this inferno that sets us alight
that chars our hands, faces, chests, and feet
rather, we dreamed of a ray of fraternal sunshine
unlocking nostalgia and an operetta of croaking frogs
must we cue up a funeral eulogy
no suicide, partial or collective, will occur today
we'll grapple with the world
until our nerves give out
dearly, we will make it pay

acceptance—
we speak the same tongue
but we struggle to understand one another
words have lost their pith
they smell of vomit or urine
drinking offers no escape
fake laughter is no better than a scowl
shall we beg for mercy from Mvidi Mukulu, the Elder Spirit
or try to communicate in an ad hoc language?
we are held accountable for our own fall
now it's time to take responsibility for the sins of the fathers

WOMB NAMES

Mwanza Tshimankinda Mukole
Kamunga wa Kamunga
Kamunga wa Mwanza
Mwanza Mujila Bisonsa
Mwamba Kabuya (Athanase)
Mwanza Mujila (Pierre)
Mwanza Mujila

THE SLAUGHTERHOUSE OF DREAMS OR THE FIRST HUMAN, BENDE'S FOLLY

kasala 78

the masquerade
or the rancid concerto
of carnivores
of carrion feeders
of cutthroats
of the first rain
keen for blood and sperm
goes on forever

kasala 22

dreams nipped in the bud?

kasala 28

the masquerade
of carnivores
blows up in our face
the masquerade
of traffickers
breeds bankruptcies
in the frail spiral
of this beautiful, broken world

kasala 11

before memory begins to play
its tricks on us
shall we spike the djudju juice
with some gin
or recite our entire genealogy
gunned down?

kasala 12

the diggers of Katekelayi
cut down in broad daylight
for having committed a single crime
mining the precious stone
in their own country
drift in the streets of Grand Kasaï

kasala 8

not even twenty suns suffice
the night continues its frantic farandole

kasala 33

the Congo River is filled to the brim
with corpses and other seeming suicides

kasala 81

should Bende, the first human, be blamed
for this charade?
if he'd known how his plotting would end
would he have dared size up Mvidi Mukulu?

kasala 29

Patrice Emery Lumumba
Rossy Mukendi Tshimanga
Floribert Chebeya
Fidèle Bazana
Thérèse Kapangala
the list of so-called suicides
is as long as the Mississippi

kasala 44

the night
still rings with the laughter
of the children of Katekelayi
a cerebral cacophony on repeat—
their breath
their ragged breathing
their seared voices—
mixing with the uproar
of others who perished during the full moon

kasala 15

because of one man: Bende
the universe went off the rails

kasala 85

the mass graves of Maluku
what a lovely story!
holes stuffed with meat
a century-old stench

kasala 64

Central Africa is a slaughterhouse

kasala 86

in the tunnels of Shinkolobwe
kids, with their pinched faces
bellies bloated from disease
dig, measles printed on their bodies
they reek of excrement and gasoline
their scrabbly, yellow teeth
scrape a bare existence from the walls
they await, without fear, the cave-in

kasala 73

we had the sun in our mouths

kasala 25

and Bende's curse sticks to our skin

kasala 68

what was Bende thinking
as he clumsily tugged on the strings?
that Mvidi would resume creation?
a second begetting
to satisfy the creature's swollen ego
a farce that dare not speak its name

kasala 51

let this be a warning
by catching epilepsy
from these sclerotic nights
forsaken by God
weaned from mother's milk
stricken with scurvy
infested with mosquitos
and other insects
we've become a nomadic people
headless, spineless
scattered in the bush
party animals in Hong Kong
boozers in Moscow
club dancers in Málaga
night watchmen in Prague
errand boys in Casablanca
carwash guys in Brazza

kasala 1

the trains still carry
kids and ore
through the backcountry of Katanga

kasala 38

it all began in Nsanga-a-Lubangu
the exodus of my Kaku and his family
other migrations followed
then the return to the mines of Katanga
then headlong flight
the skeleton balled up in pain

kasala 67

the counterfeit couples
like the cutthroats of the full moon
can think of nothing better than a good pogrom
without that, and the masquerade that follows
they grow nervous
crumple everything that comes to hand

kasala 4

the carnivores in Beni never lose their hard-on
with passion they stage
an excremental orgy

kasala 63

Central Africa's favorite spot
its mass graves
those it never tires of digging
at this rate, it may swallow all its children
half of them already totter

kasala 56

in whose cabinet of curiosities
do my Kaku's amulets gather dust?

kasala 42

since we are here
Lumumba's teeth

kasala 53

I, Mukalenga Mwanza
Mwanza Mujila Tshimankinda
Mwanza Nkongolo
Mwanza wa Tshibamba Kanyinda
Mwanza wa Mwanza
will part the ocean
for whoever will bring me
arms and legs trussed
one of these dinner-jacketed spies

kasala 14

who's got the goods
on Kalambayi's offspring?
who knows in what backwater
Mukendi's issue are lying low?
Kanjinga wa Mukendi
Mulumba wa Mukendi
Ntumba wa Mukendi
Kongolo wa Mukendi

kasala 2

and to think that not even death
can ease one's return to Mwene-Ditu

kasala 3

this nourishing land
is no longer what it once was
in the time of Tshimbalanga and Mujinga
Kabwanga and Mukengeshayi Alphonse
Mulanga Judith and Mbombo Antoinette
the land of Baloji Kabambi
is but a shrinking shadow
a barren sepulcher
spitting blood
its swollen belly barking with diamonds
the brambles twist and thicken
the trees grow stunted
the rivers silt up
worse, the waters of Lake Munkamba
our only lifeline
no longer wash clean
the stain from our hands
they smell of trouble and fire
the waters of the lake

kasala 52

desperation
loosens our tongues
our pleadings to Mvidi Mukulu
jitter in the sky
Mvidi Mukulu, we beseech you
to stop driving us to suicide in our sleep
Mvidi Mukulu, we ask you
to stop plaguing us with diarrhea
Mvidi Mukulu, we implore you
to stop unleashing famine
and her sisters-in-arms:
nausea, madness, amnesia
sleeping sickness, schistosomiasis
typhoid and measles
Mvidi, stop making beggars of us
Mvidi, stop condemning us to exile
to vicarious wandering
to pointless transhumance
to death by asphyxiation
Mvidi, do not abandon us
halfway through our unraveling
without food or even a pet
at the mercy of the cutthroats of the full moon
Mvidi Mukulu, we beseech you, Mvidi Mukulu
to repeal the lightning
to end tuberculosis
to adjourn the heat wave
to dismiss the flood
to issue a permanent injunction against malaria

kasala 45

we are here
we are here, panting
having reached the chapter of despair
Pithecanthropi
the wretched of the earth
swollen bellies
rags on our backs
bodies wasted
by primordial exile
slumped over, bodies hauled
from one region to another
as dictated by hunger
the mines
wars of liberation
and as ever
malnutrition

kasala 71

who's to blame?
us or Mvidi?
us or the Celestial Animals?
us or Bende?
we were the first
to usher in the devil-may-care dance
we were the blacksmiths
of our own perdition
the assiduous artisans
of defection
now we are left to pick up the pieces
of a collective heresy—
and incidentally an unneeded one—
first, we called Mvidi
every name under the sun
then we stopped praying
shunned the kutshipulula rite
we weren't exactly headed down a good path
we scorned the Elders
on the same impulse
we hammered down
what Kaku had built up
by the sweat of his brow
as if that was not enough
we lost control
we danced stark naked
we pounded the pavement
we uttered sarcasm, stench, invective
we flaunted ill-gotten opulence
in the midst of chaos on every corner
stunned by bottles of djudju juice
and pitchers of moonshine
we abandoned the homeland
to its own pathetic fate
exile in Saint Louis
itinerancy in Moscow
exodus to Baltimore
banishment to Prague
just like Manseba, thirty years before

kasala 40

while we wait in vain
for Mvidi to redeem us
to suspend the lightning and the fire
to dull the bakishi's fury
our best chance is to force Mvidi's hand
to entreat Mvidi
to beseech Mvidi
to drag us out
of the pit
our best chance
is to haggle with the Lesser Spirits
those who have walked with Mvidi
from the time before the Stone Age began

kasala 31

the years have pulverized memory
they've ground it into laughable dust
who remembers Mujinga wa Tshimankinda
Tshisungu Mutamba, or even Lwamba François
son of the late, lamented Lwamba Jonas and Ntumba Bernadette?
Lwamba the giant
Lwamba the caterpillar eater
Lwamba, hands hardened by the pickaxe
Lwamba, lighter on his feet than a gazelle
Lwamba, burlier than a rhinoceros at the watering hole
Lwamba of the hoarse voice
Lwamba, the first to leave Mbuji-Mayi
(which means "goat-water" or "water-goat")
climbing aboard the first locomotive
in search of his umpteenth chore
in the slag heaps of Katanga
at the height of his eighteen years
Lwamba who roamed throughout the colony
Lwamba who stayed two months in Stanleyville
Lwamba who called the shots in Banningville
Lwamba and his endless trips to Thysville
Lwamba the pilgrim

Lwamba the explorer
Lwamba the mapper of the backcountry
Lwamba and his restless feet that never cramped up
Lwamba who sent the whole world packing
Lwamba who pushed logic to its limits
Lwamba who pilloried the holy rollers, the gigolos and their nephews
Lwamba who danced the rumba in the bistros of Leopoldville
Lwamba who toiled with the first whites to arrive in the country
Lwamba, valet for the Italians
Lwamba, driver for the Belgians
Lwamba, gardener for the Portuguese
Lwamba and his Greek friends
Lwamba who whispered secrets in the Americans' ears
Lwamba who knew the inside of a colonial prison
and the splendid jails of the Second Republic
Lwamba, yes, still Lwamba
Lwamba and his dynasty
Lwamba, three times shambuyi
first pregnancy:
Lwamba and his wife had two girls
second pregnancy:
Lwamba and his wife
had a girl and a boy
third pregnancy:
Lwamba and his wife
had a boy and a girl
Lwamba, the male with 67 grandchildren
Lwamba, the man who lived into his one hundred and twenty-second year
Lwamba the patriarch
Lwamba and his bluffing
Lwamba and his head-scratching gossip
Lwamba who read and wrote in the language of the Europeans
Lwamba and his supreme euphoria when he got his first bike
Lwamba, still Lwamba, posing beside his first car

kasala 36

who recalls
Mulowayi wa Kalala François
the much-nicknamed uncle—
the Ancestor
the Golden Voice
the Chief
the Warrior?
solitude, you draw us back
to the time of Mulowayi wa Kalala
a descendant of the Tshisumpa line
exile was then but a dim lure
the carats accumulated
day followed night
and night winked out before the sun
we possessed a homeland
where we sought our way
without pissing our pants

kasala 10

Mumbu
Dilenge
Mululu
Kapolowayi
Muabi
Tree Spirits
once invoked by Tshimbalanga
the second youngest of my uncles
give us strength to subdue the sun

kasala 79

Bende's nerves cracked
and here we are floundering in the mud

kasala 65

Kongolo Kaa Mukanda, the isolato
who thought he was yanking the rug
from under Mvidi Mukulu's feet
came to at the bottom of a ravine
transformed into a snake, among reptiles
a pathetic fate
for one who once was a Great Lord

kasala 83

were it not for Bende's embezzlements
we might still be in heaven above
cozier than ever

kasala 74

the tragedy of Kongolo Kaa Mukanda is to have been
from his very apparition neither Man, nor Thing, nor Animal
is that reason enough to covet other creatures
to shout oneself hoarse for an artificial beauty?
What happens next, we well know

kasala 17

country of surfeit and excess: diamonds, oil, forests, rivers, copper, mass graves

kasala 87

let's leave the creature
to his homely ruminations

kasala 88

don't think we'll rush for the exits
go wake up Kabambi Baloji Mutambayi Mwena Shabanza, Mukua Mulumba
just because Bende shot himself in the neck
or went on another bender for the umpteenth time
this week

kasala 89

the city, a public flophouse, puts on airs
the streets are awash with children
high on diamba or other drugs
who sleep in cardboard boxes and live hard
they sport the same plague-stricken faces
as their cousins grubbing underground in Shinkolobwe

kasala 90

biso nionso toza bikelemu ya Nzambe
whoever outdoes the others in disbelief
can go make their own planet
with its sex workers, its rivers, its pampas, its filth, its pimps
its mass graves, its midlife crises
its latrines, its shit shows, and all the rest

kasala 92

a poor bedfellow?
Bende gulps down moonshine
without feeling the slightest buzz
the zealot burps and struts through the crowd
he forgets he's just a puppet
a shit, nothing more

kasala 93

let's steer clear of the King of the Animals
lest we end up peopling his pantry

kasala 95

you could give Bende centuries to repent
the outcome wouldn't change
give or take a few soundbites
the same legendary shenanigans and the birth of brats

kasala 69

every creation is a form of consolation
including our own
overcome by pity, Mvidi made the Spirits (hermaphrodites)
Animals, Things, and Humans
what happens next, we well know—
a bloodbath

kasala 91

mass graves have a bright future
the clowns doze, Kalashnikovs under the pillow

kasala 105

it would be too good to be true
if they tumbled from the window with their bags of vile tricks
a leech, can you picture it eating pizza
even in your dreams?
it'd be like mistaking the ocean for the Kalahari

kasala 5

we struggle to unhear
the cries of the Katekelayi diggers

kasala 76

Mulunda wanyi
your children are still digging mass graves
punish us with dysentery or floodwaters
they've been digging for twenty years straight

kasala 39

Ntete
Tshiame
Mukulumpe
ancestors of the first dawn
if you showed yourselves to us
we might find our way out of the Zairean woods

kasala 82

the country's longest cemetery
stretches from Lubumbashi to Mbuji-Mayi
thousands of bodies crammed under the tracks
a corridor of ethnic cleansing
at every station, the trains stopped
to unload the corpses
if you're looking for the graves—
assuming they're still visible to the naked eye—
of Kabeya Jean, Mujinga Marie or even Kaniki Alphonse
catch the train from Mwene-Ditu or Katanga

kasala 54

the bakishi keep a close watch over me
rejoice in my antics
almost lose faith
uncork epilepsy and syphilis
come to their senses at the last second

kasala 49

winter is fast approaching
and my Kaku is gone

kasala 58

in his rocking chair
Kaku, my great-grandfather
looks even older
as old as the river
as ancient as the Lubumbashi–Mwene-Ditu railroad

kasala 59

Kaku can no longer use his legs
only his jaws work
he mouths forgotten names
one after the other

kasala 60

Mvidi Mukulu wa Mukulumpe
Mvidi Mukulu wa Bende
Mvidi Mukulu wa Tshiana Tshikulu
Mvidi Mukulu wa Tshilele
Mvidi Mukulu wa Tshiame
truly, I am your creature
with a toad spinning in my head
credit my deep dives in the djudju juice

kasala 84

the bakishi are still fuming
about my body pitted with smallpox
is Bende to blame?

kasala 41

the descendants of Mwanza Nkongolo
are not used to a shortage of masks
is Bende to blame?

kasala 61

kids gasping for air in a copper mine
they stagger about like zombies
is Bende to blame?

kasala 94

ba meli, ba tondi, ba buaki ngunda
Aunt Konde should kick herself
if the kids cut the cord
is Bende to blame?

kasala 18

Kaku and I lie about
don't touch a drop the entire evening
no beer, no djudju juice, not even tshibuku
the masks, the masks
is Bende to blame?

kasala 46

even if old age keeps Kaku from brawling
he seethes
upon learning the news
curses the cutthroats down to the sixth generation
cedes to collective reproach
is Bende to blame?

kasala 34

every time he gets a cavity
Kaku mentions Lumumba's teeth
is Bende to blame?

kasala 55

the diggers of Katekelayi await . . .
a resurrection, their own
is Bende to blame?

kasala 57

the cutthroats of the full moon are busy
gulp their last chalice of sperm
before rushing out for fresh meat
is Bende to blame?

kasala 47

from Nsanga-a-Lubangu
we trot behind a fictional country
is Bende to blame?

kasala 70

Mua Ntumba mourns her twins
Mbuyi and Kabanga
screaming themselves hoarse in the cells of the ANR
is Bende to blame?

kasala 26

Mwanza wa Mwanza
is still waiting for his Kaku's bracelets
is Bende to blame?

kasala 100

from our great zeal for democracy
we wound up with a country that pisses blood

kasala 98

kids barely weaned
off mothers' milk
toil in the hole
they smell of shit
is Bende to blame?

kasala 96

atop trains bound for Mbuji-Mayi
kids full to bursting with laughter
after the slag heap, will they stalk some ancestor
or summon Mvidi wa Kaku, the spirit of their foremothers
to free them from the curse
now and forever?

kasala 101

kids, bellies full of roundworms
dig by hand
in the quarries of Fungurume
is Bende to blame?

kasala 97

the masks that cross the ocean
sell for the price of knickknacks
is Bende to blame?

kasala 99

the kids keep going down the hole
they cry out to Foremother Tshiame
to spare them from a cave-in
from another bout of measles
or sleeping sickness

kasala 107

the child miners
nurse a gem of a hangover
they shave their heads
in imitation of army recruits
sport secondhand shoes
to cut a fine figure in the mines of Dimbelenge
is Bende to blame?

kasala 108

even with a gun to our heads
we won't go to Prague, Moscow, or Kingakati
but to Tshikapa instead
to perform the Tshishimbi dance
to offer nzolo to the ancestors

kasala 106

in this country where hospitals, brothels, and nursery schools
can't hold a candle to the secret police
the children who go down the hole
still dream
of digging up enough ore
to rise from the muck

kasala 102

now the children have smallpox
or is it a whiff of tuberculosis?

kasala 23

without Mvidi Mukulu wa Mukulumpe
we'd still be mired in shit
body of grimy mornings
mouths stuffed with grass

kasala 7

we won't defenestrate ourselves on the spot
no offense to the counterfeit couples

kasala 32

am I so much to be pitied
that I must be pushed into the river as a suicide?
just me or my whole line
Kaku's, that is, my great-grandfather's?

kasala 77

and if we swapped Kaku's teeth
for Lumumba's?

kasala 37

I won't line up
for a bowl of bloodstained soup
if I sell out my lineage
have Mvidi Mukulu wa Mwanza give me herpes and a heart attack
and tell the bakishi to cast me in a Cialis commercial
for the next two hundred years and forty rainy seasons

kasala 9

you may impound my hand
if it means the sun
and also the moon
will rise in my mouth
this afternoon
no offense to Bende

kasala 16

I refuse to sit down
with the cutthroats
of the first rain
they reek of fresh blood

kasala 19

I pick exile
over the cabal
no offense to Bende

kasala 20

I refuse with my belly
I refuse with my gonads
I refuse with my protozoan mug
choose madness over
dishonoring my Kaku
no offense to Bende

kasala 43

I die, my belly sliced open
oh death! The good death, what is it?
you get used to the machete
the cutthroats, the cutthroats
their passion is for the pubic mound

kasala 30

theater of the absurd?
the cutthroats of the full moon
speak of peace and love for one's neighbor
they swoon over Brahms and Mozart
yet moan when new victims are in short supply

kasala 35

I will miss Tshimbalanga forever
the second youngest of my uncles
he left to gather his share of diamonds
in the mines of Dimbelenge
is Bende to blame?

kasala 13

we scattered
according to the railway's whims
is Bende to blame?

kasala 110

what are all these jests about a pimp past his prime
is Bende to blame?

kasala 6

outlandish prices
masks sold at auction
the crowd presses in
snaps them up
is Bende to blame?

kasala 21

we had a great country
vast, green, lush, gigantic
stretching from Kinshasa to Katanga
from Luebo to Gbadolite
is Bende to blame?

kasala 72

Kongolo Kaa Mukanda wonders:
does Mvidi Mukulu ever regret
deposing me
rescinding forever my title of Great Lord
and dumping me like a criminal on Earth?

kasala 48

years after the carnage
the Katekelayi diggers rant
in the nameless tongue of the dead

kasala 109

what we do best
mass graves
shall we blame them on Bende?
has anyone actually seen him digging for us?
is it Bende who rapes the women and girls of Kivu?
is it the black hand of Bende at play in the Kamuina Nsapu massacre?
is it Bende meddling in the merry carnage of the Bundu dia Kongo faithful?
the bodies in the river, still Bende?

kasala 27

the assegais, bracelets, masks, figurines, drums, rugs, spears
and other ornaments of Mwanza wa Mwanza still loiter in the museums
is Bende to blame?

kasala 24

names are a traveling museum
when I whistle my kasala
I'm no longer alone
I'm with my mother and father
my aunts and Uncle Tshimbalanga
the Congo River and the Celestial Animals
the railroads and mountains
the sun and the rain
Munkamba Lake and the Lubilanji River
my Kaku always at my side
my Kaku and his rocking chair

my Kaku and his long beard
my bespectacled Kaku

kasala 62

this wild night
the urge to do something rash rises in my chest
I'll go dance the rumba and the Tshikuna Fou
until I snap my spine
Kaku deserves no less
than this hip-swiveling tribute to his mukishi

kasala 50

I summon 347 horses
I summon the earthquake
I summon the solar eclipse
I summon the flood
I summon the stars
I summon 560 luxury rides
I summon 345 rhinoceroses
I summon 67 tigers
I summon the Mississippi, I summon the Maningoza, I summon the Maroni, I summon the Brahmaputra, I summon the Okavango and the Jordan and the Niger and the Saloum and the Essequibo and the Euphrates and the Mackenzie and the Rio Grande and the Kamchatka and the Yangtze and the Santa Cruz and the Suriname and the Amu Darya and the Ganges and the Congo and the Indus and the Charente and the Dnieper and the Dordogne and the Irrawaddy and the Guadalquivir and the Meuse and the Volga and the Mokau and the Sepik and the Tiber and the Yser and the Lena and the Tanganyika and the Orinoco and the Mekong and the Tshangalele and the Danube and the Amazon and the Rhine and the Limmat and the Nile and the Limpopo and the Zambezi
to celebrate a Woman
my mother, Ma'Nanga

THE CITY WITHIN

don't say I've lost my cabeza
I'm not to blame
blame the city
that rumbles in my belly
(and saddles me with seizures)
every time I mention it
. . . my inner city is a squatters' city, a contraband city
a forbidden city, a humongous slum
derelict yet self-assured
everyone is welcome here
no visas or vaccination cards required
and in my city, the racists, nativists
and cutthroats of the full moon are sent packing
they defenestrate themselves into the sea
if they aren't inclined to put up with our laughter and smells
our parties and yen for freedom, our bebop and rumba
a world without skylights is a dim utopia
and we know where utopias tend when they float
last-minute heresies and hoaxes
don't say I've lost my cabeza
my inner city is a happy city
my inner city is a cosmopolitan city
my inner city is a crossroads of civilizations
my inner city sits between East and West
the African tropics and Central Europe
Latin America and South Sudan
Bolivia and Afghanistan
long thoroughfares connect every neighborhood of the city
my city
(por favor)
don't say I've lost my cabeza
don't say it, even to Mvidi Mukulu, the Elder Spirit
. . . my inner city is the most populous in the world
but also the most carnal and brotherly

people lay the table and eat outdoors
under the noonday sun
they roll in laughter
in my city, the doors and windows of the apartments
are open wide all year long to the traveler, passerby and chance caller
the seasons clot in a mad desire for redemption
wet summers, mild winters
don't say I've lost my cabeza
. . . my inner city is a port city
it dips its feet and hair in the water
thousands of berths and embarkations take place all over my city
bringing salt, apples, cherries, silk
rugs, rum, djudju juice, shells
rice wine as well as humans in all shapes and sizes
expressing themselves in various languages unknown even to them
on each face a genealogy etched
by years of migration and seasonal travels . . .
don't say I've lost my cabeza
or that it's only tooth decay that loosens my tongue
my inner city, the city of Mwanza Mujila
is a conglomerate of dreams
and some of these dreams are green, sumptuous, thunderous
my city is a veranda, an enormous bazaar, a fair
a baffling jukebox, an open-air bar, a marvelous bordello
here we play and make swing every kind of music
and dance: tango, polka piqué, candombe
the waltz, samba, kizomba and nonstop jazz
when you pace the alleyways of my city
of my inner city, if you don't hear Mingus on bass
Mongezi Feza on trumpet, Max Roach on drums
Dudu Pukwana on sax, Duke Ellington on piano
it's because the vibratos of Bessie Smith pulse in your ears
a feverish voice singing crazy love a cappella
between the Angelus and the muezzin's call to prayer
shh! don't say I've lost my cabeza
three emancipated rivers flow through my city:
the Yangtze, the Danube and the Limpopo
my city is fragrant with daffodils, the scents
and spices of Zanzibar
my inner city is a city of hope

my inner city is not a citadel
my inner city is not a prison
my inner city begins in Graz
and ends in Port Elizabeth
passing through Caracas, Nagoya, Thessaloniki
Odessa and Seattle
in my inner city, I am not some guy from the Congo
or Zimbabwe
in my inner city, I am not a man
I am not a woman
in my inner city, I am not a black
I am not a foreigner
in my inner city, I am not a black
I am not a white
in my inner city, I am not a black
in my inner city, I am not a black
in my inner city, I am not a black
in my inner city, I am just the grandson
of my paternal grandmother, Julienne Mwa Mwanza

VIRTUES

moderation—
raving madmen of the first rain
first we collared the sun
held its head underwater
until it drowned in the river
what coup have we not attempted?
no doubt, we'll finish with toothless gums
bloated bellies
and bodies pickled by snail fever
once too often the pitcher
goes to the well
better to dismember
ourselves
snuff out this life of debauchery

tolerance—
we've been unsuitable in every sense
eternal mama's boys and total narcissists
smooth talkers, unrepentant boors
we shimmied naked under the noonday sun
flaunting our genitalia like spoils of war
oiling pedestrians with our spit and snot
revolting, exceptionally nervous
not ones to rest on our laurels
we slashed and burned the sun
our only salvation: to abstain!

joy—
one evening I'll wake from my long years of leprous slumber
I'll draw myself a warm bath and soak for hours on end
later on, I'll button up my best shirt
and go dance the rumba
until my muscles say "no more"
I'll dance for the children gesticulating

in the diamond mines
I'll toe-tap the flamenco
and the pachanga for Syria, Somalia, and Iraq
timing my tremolos with the clanging
of the cymbals, the sax, the bass clarinet

PANDEMONIUM BAZAAR

for a trumpet player

we are dozens
hundreds, maybe millions, to bear these names
the same prostheses unaltered since the Stone Age
the same almost unpronounceable knickknacks
the same lemony syllables
tapping out distant lands
dislocated geographies
in the meanders of collective memory

names that—
like a cross leaning on an untended grave—
evoke villages vaccinated at a dizzying pace
sixty-two bombs a day
villages of mutilated buildings
villages nipped in the bud
starving villages
cholera-stricken villages
rendered without warning as silent as the grave!
villages with shrunken, bloodless dreams
cut off from paradise
disfigured villages
smashed-in villages
spectral villages
without electricity or running water
forsaken by god and at the mercy of jihadists
and other featherbrained fighters
without faith or moral compass, obsessed with nothing
but kicking life in the teeth

we are many in this pathetic spectacle
dozens, hundreds, or millions bearing the same fates
(some of us submitting to this macabre exercise

since the psychedelic dawn of the poor old world)
mastering our fright and scrambling
to scale the Aegean or that other sea they call the Mediterranean—
even if it means strewing these waters with our corpses—
dreaming of passing through Turkey, Hungary, Slovenia, or Siberia
in the hope of reaching France or the Swedish capital
not even knowing where our legs take us
the main thing being to make landfall

we are hundreds
fear in the belly
moving mechanically
in mildewed skins
rags on our backs
carrying, on this endless march
what remains of our native lands: a parrot's song, an evening dance, a smile, the scent of tea, a mother's face, the memory of an absent brother...

we are hundreds at the door
we knock and will keep knocking until our voices reach you
repeating that we've been here since cockcrow
waiting for this, or some other city, to receive us

we are millions, stationed in Greece
parked in Libya, or stalled in Turkey
fondling the same guava-flavored trifles
eyes on the stars
enamored with hope
determined to survive
braving fatigue and braving illness and braving thirst and braving the winter chill, the storms, the prison guards, and anarchy and braving the sun
until we can no longer feel our hands
and lose the use of our eyes and genitals and tongues and noses and left knees
until we begin to hallucinate, until we fantasize
about a world without guns, until we unspool
dreams at such heights
that by multiplying, they restore dignity
to all beings and things

from marching through rain and sunlight
snow and mire
loneliness and hope
we grow dizzy
and, as a result, we lose our connections to machines and ourselves
we no longer know who we are
from what meat we are made
or from what family tree we descend
in short, what our mores were and if we have
always been human

the earth no longer swivels about the sun
it jams up, or switches off, depending upon who takes your call
and the sundering of yesterday's space condemns us to an exile
without return

if, by accident, we realize we live
in a severe, almost cerebral utopia
we still do not know how to fish our skulls from the waters
since perhaps a maritime metaphor is needed
to affix a correct anatomy to this disarray
let's try this one: we are figurines in the middle of a storm-tossed sea
or this one: water penetrates us through the mouth, ears, and nose
let's repeat this one: the shipwreck is obviously grand

the dogs join the concerto
every chance we get, we howl late into the night
but nothing edible springs to life
from this cacophony set up as a mode of governance

everything splits apart
in a devastating surge, and we, still millions of us
try to reckon
where to place the last words of this pandemonium bazaar
that is the world

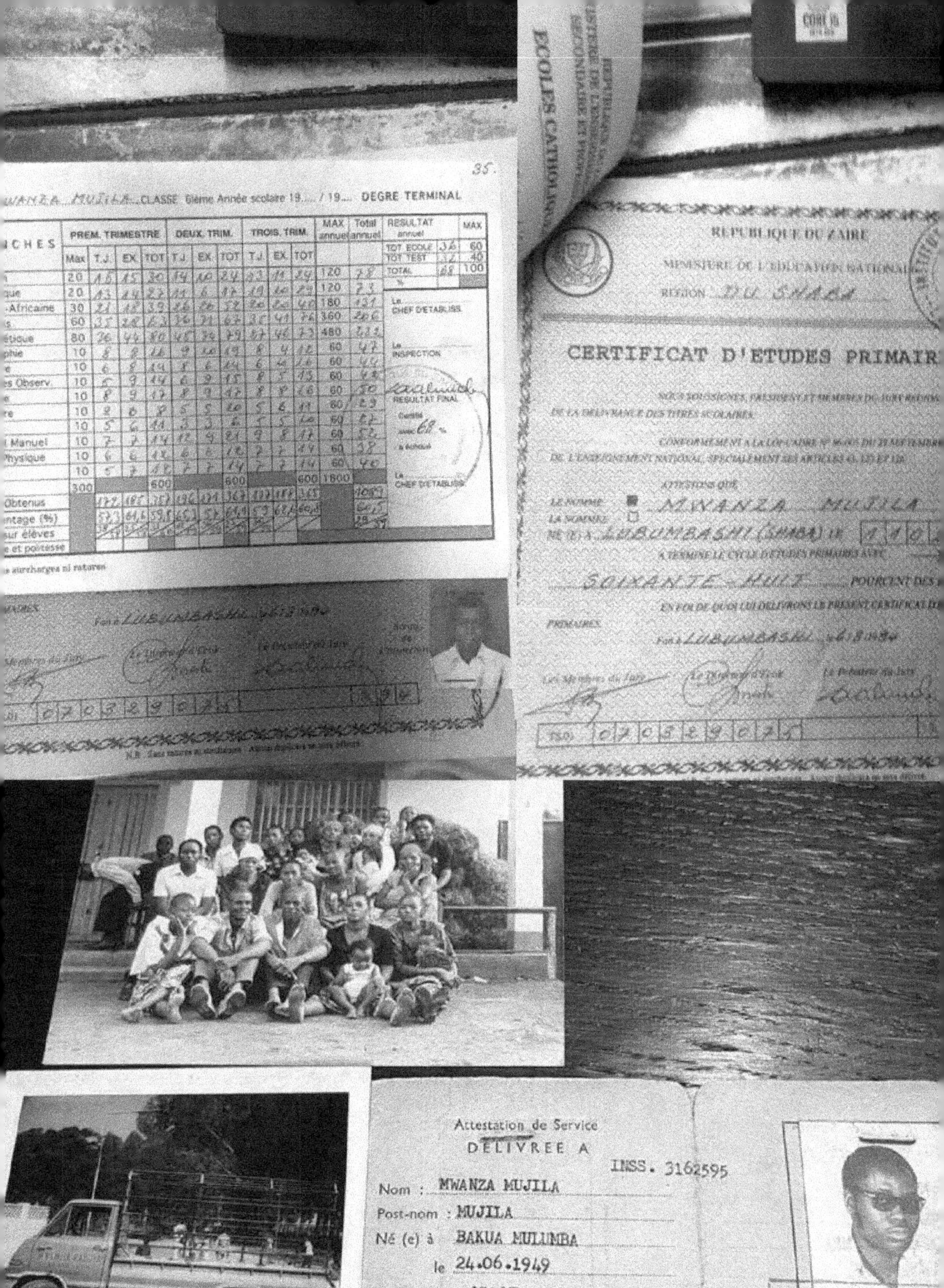

ECOLES CATHOLIQUES
REPUBLIQUE DU ZAIRE
MINISTERE DE L'EDUCATION NATIONALE
REGION DU SHABA
CERTIFICAT D'ETUDES PRIMAIRES
MWANZA MUJILA
LUBUMBASHI (SHABA)
SOIXANTE-HUIT
LUBUMBASHI
DEGRE TERMINAL
PREM. TRIMESTRE
DEUX. TRIM.
TROIS. TRIM.
RESULTAT FINAL
Attestation de Service
DELIVREE A
INSS. 3162595
Nom : MWANZA MUJILA
Post-nom : MUJILA
Né (e) à BAKUA MULUMBA
le 24.06.1949
Fils(fille) de MWAMBA KABUYA
Nationalité : ZAIROISE
Profession : GERANT COMMERCIAL
MARIE
Zone : KATUBA
Formule dactyl. : 44443-44242-1332-13
S.D. : 511/244.771
Fait à Lubumbashi, le 5.1.1976
LUBUMBASHI

REPUBLIQUE DU ZAIRE
PRIMAIRES
TS01
NOM MWANZA MUJILA
CLASSE 5 ans

Notes

J. Bret Maney

KASALA FOR MYSELF 1

kasala: a traditional form of oral praise poetry practiced by the Luba people of the southern Democratic Republic of Congo. In *Le chant kasàlà des Luba* (Julliard, 1968), Patrice Mufuta describes the kasala as "a free-verse poem made up of praise-names. It is sung or recited in an elevated tone, in public settings . . . It is intended to elicit yearning and is sometimes performed with musical accompaniment." Originally composed in Tshiluba, the kasala was adapted for French in the 1960s by the important Congolese poet and scholar Clémentine Faïk-Nzuji.

For Fiston Mwanza Mujila, the orality of the traditional kasala survives in the improvisatory freedom of the performer. "If I recite my poem," he once told me, "it will end up being longer because I'm going to improvise or choose variations from the main text." This extensibility—some critics have charted instances of the kasala extending past eight hundred lines—prompts Mwanza Mujila to note similarities with the blues or jazz, an artistic kinship made explicit in the jazz-suffused soundscape of the final stanza of "Kasala for Myself 1."

Ma'Nanga: a nickname for the poet's mother, derived from her family name, Nanga.

Indépendance cha-cha: a reference to the song of the same name debuted by Joseph Kabasele and his group African Jazz at the 1960 Belgo–Congolese Round Table Conference in Brussels, during which the terms of Congolese independence were negotiated. In a year defined by decolonial struggles across the continent, the song became a major Pan-African hit.

KASALA FOR MYSELF 2

Mwanza Mbala . . . Mwanza Nkangi . . . Mwanza Nkongolo: In Luba cosmology, the mingled breath of the male snake (mwanza mbala) and female snake (mwanza nkangi) creates the rainbow (mwanza-nkongolo) that marks the end of the rainy season, thereby rescuing humanity. In a poem of self-praise, "Mwanza," the poet's surname, can be read as a diminutive of "Mwanza Nkongolo," the rainbow.

KASALA FOR MY KAKU 1

Kaku: a respectful designation in Tshiluba for a grandparent or great-grandparent. Upon their death, Kaku becomes a spirit capable of intervening in the affairs of the living.

Mwanza wa Mwanza: Mwanza, descendant of Mwanza

first war in Shaba: Shaba I, or "La première guerre du Shaba" in French, was a 1977 armed conflict in Katanga province, then known as Shaba, pitting Zaire's military against rebels crossing the border from Angola.

the massacre of the Katekelayi diggers: a reference to the mass killing of artisanal diamond miners in Katekelayi, in Eastern Kasaï province, in 1979, which provoked national and international condemnation.

the Second Republic: name euphemistically given to Mobutu Sese Seko's regime (1965–1997). The turbulent First Republic lasted from 1960–1965.

KASALA FOR MY KAKU 2

Mvidi Mukulu: "Elder Spirit" or "Supreme Being," a reference to God.

BEFORE THE BANISHMENT

Foremother Tshiame: an important early female ancestor venerated by the Luba.

Mikombo wa Kalewa: A character variously taken up in Luba origin stories, the epithet can also designate a name of God.

KASALA 81

Bende: a highly polysemous word in Tshiluba: 1. When not used as a proper noun, "bende" can serve to indicate possession. For example, "mbuji wa bende," someone else's goat. 2. "Bende" is a name of God since Bende occupies a privileged place in the divine lineage, and God is frequently invoked together with the names of illustrious persons. 3. Bende refers to the ancestor of all human beings. 4. Bende refers to the human ancestor brought into creation in the form of the twin, or couple, formed by one man and one woman. 5. In genealogies, Bende is also identified as one of the founders of the clan, or *bakole*. 6. Bende appears in legends as the equal or double of God. Bende orchestrates the world with God but also contradicts their authority (see R. van Caeneghem, *La notion de Dieu chez les baLuba du Kasaï*, 1956) [author's note].

KASALA 29

Patrice Emery Lumumba: independence leader and first prime minister of the independent Democratic Republic of Congo (DRC), murdered in 1961.

Rossy Mukendi Tshimanga: a pro-democracy, Catholic activist and university professor murdered by police during a protest in Kinshasa in 2018.

Floribert Chebeya: executive director of the Congolese human rights organization Voice of the Voiceless, murdered after a 2010 meeting at police headquarters in Kinshasa.

Fidèle Bazana: Floribert Chebeya's driver and a member of Voice of the Voiceless, Bazana was abducted at the same time as Chebeya. His body has never been recovered.

Thérèse Kapangala: novice nun murdered by police on the steps of her church in Kinshasa in 2018 during a pro-democracy demonstration.

KASALA 85

the mass graves of Maluku: During the night of March 19, 2015, security forces buried at least 420 bodies in a mass grave in Maluku, a municipality in the Tshangu district of Kinshasa. Despite widespread calls for investigation, the identities of the deceased remain unverified.

KASALA 86

tunnels of Shinkolobwe: Located in Katanga province, the Shinkolobwe uranium mine was the primary source of uranium for the atomic bombs dropped on Hiroshima and Nagasaki by the United States in 1945. While the mine has been officially closed since 1960, today artisanal miners risk their lives by digging up cobalt, copper, and uranium at the abandoned site.

KASALA 38

Nsanga-a-Lubangu: the legendary place of origin of the Luba people, situated in Katanga, from which they migrated into the Kasaï region over a period of centuries.

KASALA 67

the counterfeit couples: In Luba cosmology, creation privileges paired or coupled elements, such as water and fire, elder and junior, sky and earth. The "faux doubles," or "counterfeit couples," denote a violation, a counterfeiting, of this divine order.

the cutthroats of the full moon: a reference to the intelligence services active during Mobutu's regime. Nicknamed "the owls," they operated at night.

KASALA 56

my Kaku's amulets: Experts estimate that more than 90% of sub–Saharan cultural artifacts are held in collections outside Africa. See Lyndel V. Prott, ed., *Witnesses to History: A Compendium of Documents and Writings on the Return of Cultural Objects*, UNESCO Publishing, 2009.

KASALA 42

Lumumba's teeth: kept as a memento by the Belgian police officer who helped dismember and dissolve in acid the body of murdered Congolese prime minister Patrice Lumumba. In 2020, a Belgian court ordered the extant tooth be returned to Lumumba's heirs.

KASALA 3

in the time of Tshimbalanga and Mujinga / Kabwanga: respectively, the author's uncle, aunt, and a childhood friend who died young. The other names cited in these lines are inventions of the author.

Baloji Kabambi: a reference to the poet's collaborator, the Congolese visual artist Sammy Baloji, whose photographs of Congolese mines are reprinted in this book. Mwanza Mujila's kasala cycle "The Slaughterhouse of Dreams or the First Human, Bende's Folly" was originally composed to accompany a 2019 art installation by Baloji, exhibited at the Museum Rietberg in Zürich, and later included in the 2020 Biennale of Sydney.

Lake Munkamba: a lake in the Kasaï region sacred to the Luba people.

KASALA 71

Celestial Animals: In Luba cosmology, God first created the heavenly order, including the Celestial Animals, which can be distinguished from the terrestrial animals created during a second phase of creation.

the kutshipulula rite: a Luba ceremony in which an offering is made to avert the harmful effects of an oath in which God's name is uttered.

Manseba: maternal uncle (Tshiluba).

KASALA 40

bakishi: in the singular, *mukishi*. The spirits or manes of the departed. Deceased relatives acquire this status and remain reference points for the living [author's note].

KASALA 31

shambuyi: a Tshiluba honorific given to the father of twins.

KASALA 65

Kongolo Kaa Mukanda: "The Lawgiver" or "The Spiral of the Law." Brother of the rain, a being who is half human, half animal, he blamed God for his imperfect appearance. Kongolo Kaa Mukanda then went further by trying to deceive God, which led to his being expelled from heaven. Tiarko Fourche and Henri Morlighem offer an extensive account of this story in *Une Bible Noire: Cosmogonie bantu* (Les Deux Océans, 2002) [author's note].

KASALA 88

Kabambi Baloji Mutambayi Mwena Shabanza, Mukua Mulumba: a reference to the visual artist Sammy Baloji, including his lineage and clan name. For more on Baloji, see the note for "Kasala 3" above.

KASALA 89

diamba: marijuana.

KASALA 90

biso nionso toza bikelemu ya Nzambe: "we are all creatures of God" (Lingala). In other words, no one can boast of having created themselves.

KASALA 93

the King of the Animals: a reference to Joseph Kabila (b. 1971), the former president of the Democratic Republic of Congo from 2001–2019, who imported wildlife to create a lavish safari park at his ranch on the outskirts of Kinshasa.

KASALA 76

Mulunda wanyi: my God (Tshiluba); the expression can also designate a friend.

KASALA 82

the country's longest cemetery: during the colonial period, the Luba of Kasaï migrated to Katanga province to work in the mines. In the 1990s, Katangese politicians stoked ethnic tensions and the Luba with roots in the Kasaï were forcibly expelled from the region, deported on slow-moving trains with little food or water. At each station, the train stopped to bury the dead. In common parlance, we say that the longest cemetery is the railway from Katanga to Kasaï [author's note].

KASALA 60

Mvidi Mukulu wa Mukulumpe, etc.: The title "Mvidi Mukulu" ("Elder Spirit") is often combined with other names, including those of illustrious persons, in order to underline one of God's attributes. Many reverential forms of address arise in this way.

KASALA 94

ba meli, ba tondi, ba buaki ngunda: "they drink, eat well, and apply for asylum" (Lingala).

KASALA 18

tshibuku: a beer brewed from fermented corn.

KASALA 70

ANR: French acronym for the Agence Nationale de Renseignements, the name under which the repressive Congolese national intelligence agency has been known since 1997 when Laurent-Désiré Kabila became head of state.

KASALA 108

Kingakati: the site of former president Joseph Kabila's ranch and safari park, which he made his principal residence after leaving office in 2019.

Tshikapa: city in the Kasaï where the first diamond was "discovered," provoking a mining rush in the region.

the Tshishimbi dance: traditional dance practiced by the Luba in which the dancers engage in ritual insults and verbal jousting.

Nzolo: hen (Tshiluba).

KASALA 21

from Kinshasa to Katanga / from Luebo to Gbadolite: four place names roughly mapping the cardinal points of the nation. Gbadolite, to the north, is Mobutu's ancestral village where he built a palace known as the "African Versailles," a much-rued symbol of his kleptocratic regime.

KASALA 109

rapes the women and girls of Kivu: Since the advent of the Kivu conflict, in the eastern part of the country, security forces and combatants have used rape and sexual violence against women and girls as a pervasive tool of war.

the Kamuina Nsapu massacre: deadly conflict in the Kasaï region from 2016–2019, pitting repressive government forces against a local Luba militia.

carnage of the Bundu dia Kongo faithful: a separatist religious movement in the Bas-Congo made up of members of the Kongo ethnic group. More than two hundred Bundu dia Kongo followers have been killed in clashes with police since 2002.

KASALA 62

the Tshikuna Fou: a derivative of mutuashi, a traditional Luba dance emphasizing the dancer's hip movements.

THE CITY WITHIN

cabeza: head (Spanish).

por favor: please (Spanish).

“The Child of Zaire”: A Conversation with Fiston Mwanza Mujila on the Kasala and His Art of Memory

Interviewed by Antoine Wauters and J. Bret Maney

Antoine Wauters: In all your books, starting with *Tram 83*, the reader gets the feeling that you explode time and its units of measure. In *The Slaughterhouse of Dreams*, when you evoke your Kaku, you make him 105, 120, 186, even 200 years old. Where does this desire to blow up time come from? Is it a way of poking fun or of mockery? A method for playing down time's importance?

Fiston Mwanza Mujila: In Tshiluba, “Kaku” is an honorific referring to your grandparent. The grandparent in my poem “Kasala for My Kaku 1” was actually a woman, my father's grandmother. When I was a child, I found her extraordinary longevity to be so confusing that I mistakenly thought she was a man. During the writing of this book, I decided, in good faith, to experiment with this ambiguity.

Mpinda, which was her name, was born at the beginning of the twentieth century, perhaps even much earlier. This fact is a boon for the writer I became. I use literature to fill in the blank spaces and what is left unsaid in the memory of our family and clan. The same approach applies to the Congo, which is a colonial invention, just like Africa.

In my books, I allow myself to cover my tracks. I make use of my subjectivity and the marginality that has defined my career to interrogate and deconstruct Western temporalities. I am the son, grandson, and great-grandson of the colonized. I was born in the mining city of Lubumbashi. I unpacked my suitcases in Graz more than a decade ago. These two cities—marginal in relation to Vienna, Paris, or Kinshasa—constitute my observation posts.

In my grandparents' home, two cultural spheres coexisted. These two worlds alternately clashed or intermingled. While my paternal grandparents were hardly champions of the French language, they did want their grandchildren to have a perfect command of the language of the whites—*mwakulu wa batoka*. Grandfather had done many odd jobs for the Europeans before striking out on his own. When he saw us speaking French, there was wonder and even worry in his eyes.

Returning to the question of age, as far back as I go in my childhood, I do not recall my grandfather or even my grandmother ever celebrating their birthdays. They hardly mentioned them. Nor did they assign the least importance to my own. Like Kaku of blessed memory, they belonged to a generation that had lived through the brutal contact of the West with Africa. In the Congolese writer and philosopher V. Y. Mudimbe's book *The Invention of Africa*, he captures this situation in three phases: "the domination of physical space, the reformation of natives' minds, and the integration of local economic histories into the Western perspective."

Did my grandfather not know his birthday? Was he uncertain of it? I have no idea. His behavior reflected what was probably his refusal to adjust to the new paradigm of civil status [*l'état civil*]. I always feel a twinge in my heart when I fill out administrative documents. There really isn't enough space to write my full name. What about my grandfather who had as many names as there are stars in the sky?

The boycotting of Western ideas about time and age could also explain the nicknames that family elders gave me. They called me by the names of ancestors in our family tree. Through this process, I became their elder, older even than my father and mother, which was a catastrophe. I would get furious whenever I was called Mwanza wa Mwanza, Mwanza Tshimankinda Mukole, Mwanza Mujila Bisonsa, and so on. I was about five or six years old. I was just learning to write my name, to read, to draw a giraffe . . . I did not grasp then the significance of these nomenclatures. I hated them.

Wauters: You write, "I decided to remain the child of Zaire." Tell me about your relationship to this country, formerly Zaire, today the Congo?

Mwanza Mujila: In the Congo, we underwent an acceleration of history. The country wrested its independence from Belgium in June 1960. In the immediate aftermath, we lived through the secession of several provinces, the 1961 assassination of Patrice Lumumba, followed by the mysterious death of the Secretary General of the United Nations. Then Mobutu, who seized power in 1965, launched his authenticity campaign, a political ideology aiming at the erasure of colonial memory: the river, the currency, and the country now all bore the flamboyant name of Zaire, as did the cities, which took African names. Mobutu proclaimed himself Field Marshal and reigned supreme until his ouster, in 1997, during the rebellion mounted by Laurent-Désiré Kabila. The country became the Congo again, the currency and the river as well. The new strongman of Kinshasa was assassinated after another couple of years. His son ascended to the throne and led the country, not without a heaping spoonful of autocracy, while, in the background, there were rebellions, mass killings, chaotic elections.

I am struck by a sense of waste, tinged with fragile hope, every time I mention my country. The image that comes to mind is one of an extremely generous, maternal woman. Every morning she gives birth to incomparably beautiful children. But as soon as evening falls, she rushes to drown them in the ocean. We make up a huge crowd, those that this country has forced into exile, into debasement, into vice . . . Without false modesty, one can say that the Congo is a dashed paradise. As large as Western Europe, it boasts arable land, endless minerals, hydroelectric potential that ranks among the world's greatest, forests and volcanoes . . . yet its people still live hand to mouth.

I am in the habit of comparing the Congo to the condition of Austria and Germany just after the Second World War. I identify with the writers of the immediate postwar period (*Nachkriegsliteratur*), such as those of Gruppe 47, who sought to renew literature and the writer's contract in relation to an exsanguine society.

Being a Congolese writer is no joke. In this country massacres on a large scale are still a regular occurrence in the East, and no one bats an eye. There is, in addition, the obvious situation of writing in a former colonial language from the vantage point of exile, even if voluntary, about a nation in ruins. The Congo forged my literary identity. Here, I would like to borrow the words of Ilse Aichinger: "*Der Krieg hat die Dinge geklärt.*" Put otherwise, war makes the world more intelligible.

Wauters: Do you, as a writer, feel the pull of homesickness? For your childhood? Or for a distant time when everything was unified? I ask you this because of the prominent place of the Luba people in this collection, the Luba whose kingdom was among the first to be established in the Congo basin, around the fifteenth century of our era.

Mwanza Mujila: More than homesickness, I'd say that my writing attempts to reconstruct memory through an artistic process. For me, memory can be understood according to the paradigm of Jan Assmann. In his best-known work, *Cultural Memory and Early Civilization*, the German Egyptologist Assmann establishes a clear difference between communicative memory and what he calls cultural memory. The first, which is informal in nature, is based on memories of a recent past that the subject shares with people around him. It does not survive beyond three to four generations. Communicative memory includes biographical experiences and typically fades with the disappearance of those who carry it. Cultural memory, on the other hand, concerns origin stories and is maintained or archived by specialists: poets, griots, bards, etc.

My paternal grandfather, who was never one to be at a loss for words—unlike his wife—embodied both types of memory. When he died in 2008, I had already left the country. His passing came as a shock to me. I surveyed the damage caused by his death. I understood that a world was gone forever. I remembered how, during my childhood, he used to wax eloquent about his travels between the regions of Kasaï and Katanga as well as about family history—the comings and goings of this person or that, their marriages, and so on—but at the time, I took no interest in such matters.

I was born in Katanga, the mining region famous for its copper. My ancestors are from the region of Kasaï. During the colonial period, they migrated to the South to labor in the mines. The Union Minière du Haut-Katanga had just been founded. Brawn was needed to keep the machine turning. A vast recruitment campaign was launched throughout the Belgian colony, in southern Africa, in Rwanda, and in Burundi. It was amid this gold rush atmosphere that my grandparents settled in Katanga. They moved there with their culture. With them, I spoke only Tshiluba.

In this collection, I am in conversation with myself. I revive memories of adored family members like my aunts Mbuyi and Ntumba or my uncle Tshimbalanga; I examine signal events in the history of the Luba people, such as the massacre of the Katekelayi diggers; I evoke cultural practices like the Tshishimbi dance. There are also ample spiritual and cosmological themes. To nourish these poems, I was inspired by the writings of Tiarko Fourche and Henri Morlighem as well as the Luba oral tradition. Over the past few years, my poems have become more genealogical. Poetry is the permanent search for meaning. This might explain the genealogical turn in my work.

Structurally and thematically, the influence of the kasala genre is prominent.

A form of orature, the kasala is a poem or song that knits together the events of the community. The recourse to fiction is not prohibited. A kasala may be addressed to a loved one, a historical figure, or even a fictional character. In March 2021, at my father's funeral, many women—cousins, nieces, aunts, and even my mother—were transformed into storytellers. Between sobs, they recorded the trajectory of Mwanza Mujila in family and ancestral lore.

J. Bret Maney: Your kasala are genealogical, replete with ancestors' names and lineages, but they are also populated by nameless children. These children's lives are defined by their brevity, their stolen childhoods, their labor in the mines, illnesses, and famine. The collection further recalls the pogroms and deportations of the Luba in the 1990s, their expulsion from Katanga back to the Kasaï region of their ancestors. The Kasaï itself, you write, "is but a shrinking shadow" relative to its past. How did you rework the traditional kasala form to negotiate this asymmetry between past and present, between praise and mourning, between venerated ancestors and the truncated lives of these suffering, anonymous children?

Mwanza Mujila: The kasala has always provided a magnificent window onto an ancient world to the extent that the poet or singer has the talent necessary to throw themselves into the lived experience or remote past of a character (living, deceased, or fictional). When memory fails, to move their audience, or for the sole beauty of words, the poet invents. Their job is to braid a link between a buried world and the one that is being created. I am not remaking a world through my affiliation with this cultural practice. In fact, I do not adhere strictly to all of the conventions of the kasala. Doing so would be exceedingly difficult, even impossible, since the kasala is rooted in the language, imagination, and culture of the Luba people, while, for my part, I write in French.

As a form of oratory, the kasala includes multiple themes that can be juxtaposed or overlap. Even when reciting a narrative of grief, the singer (*mwena kasala*) can praise the deceased to the point of heroizing him—by amplifying his qualities, attributing to him new abilities, registering his name in a network of remarkable figures.

Let's return to *The Slaughterhouse of Dreams*. It is above all a book of mourning. I began writing it when I learned that my father had cancer and that his days were numbered. I finished it a few days before he made his final voyage. In the Congo—and probably elsewhere, what do I know?—when people go to the cemetery for a burial, they take the opportunity to visit (to say hello) and stand before the tombs of their loved ones, relatives, and acquaintances. When women or men perform a kasala at a gravesite, they evoke, by extension, other deceased persons, the lives they led and the circumstances of their deaths. Death therefore becomes a collective event. In this poetry collection, the sickness and imminent death of my father was a starting point for me for remembering others who had perished, sometimes under circumstances of unspeakable violence, such as the miners I write about and the victims of different wars or Mobutu's dictatorship . . . This is a book of personal, familial, and national mourning. I remember victims without limiting myself to any fixed temporality. The kasala here serves as a site of memory—not necessarily a political act. It is first and foremost for me and mine that I sing. I try to give a face, a voice, a trace to all those whom History passes over in silence. It is no secret that the Congo today is a dystopia, if not a gigantic abattoir. It is in this context that I recall the ethnic cleansing of the Luba people in Katanga in the 1990s. This Congolese tragedy (like others, before and after) is downplayed, excluded, even banished from collective memory.

Wauters: I want to ask about how all of this relates to your style as a reader of poetry. The first time I heard you read your work was an unforgettable experience. It was in Paris, at the Société des Gens de Lettres. After somewhat shyly answering the moderator's questions, you took the microphone and launched into an ecstatic, almost trance-like reading, full of furious laughter and gasps. Do you also write this way? By hurling forth your verses? As if to break something? How do you explain this state of "going out" of yourself?

Mwanza Mujila: The Lubumbashi Swahili expression *Ndjina ya mu tumbo* (womb name) indicates the family name, which precedes the birth of the child. Family names are organized like a museum space, with the main difference being that the artifacts—the names and the persons who incarnate them—remain alive. Names actualize all the eponymous members of a family. When I perform my poetry, my whole lineage joins in the exercise. I have the impression that I am reading with my parents; my brothers and sisters; my favorite aunts, Ntumba and Mbuyi; the second youngest of my uncles, Tshimbalanga, who departed in the '90s to search for diamonds in the Kasaï; my uncle Katumbayi, in spite of his overfondness for the bottle; and many others. On stage, my voice is electrified. Suddenly, I become a river, a crowd, a country, a world.

I'm not the first nor will I be the last to carry within me voices and bodies that are not mine. An anecdote, by way of illustration: several years ago, I asked a village elder—Lubanza by name—to recite my family's genealogy. He uttered two sentences in Swahili before switching to Tshiluba, his native tongue. He seemed in the grip of a hallucination. His vocal timbre shifted to a higher pitch. His face became drawn. He started to sweat. His hands and feet shook. When he finally stopped talking, he was out of breath. He ordered me to bring him something to drink and changed the subject of conversation. I could sense that he had relived in his body the events that he had convoked: the illnesses and deaths of my family's important ancestors, the births, marriages, accidents, and childhoods, the train journeys made during the colonial era by certain aunts and cousins . . .

To answer your question, when I perform a genealogical poem or any text, I come into mental correspondence with my subject, even if the latter is fictional. The laughter, gestures, tremolos, and imitations are part of this. I would add that there is nothing therapeutic in this exercise. Poetry is, for me, a spiritual phenomenon. And each performance is a rite. I communicate with the trees, the ancestors, the departed. As soon as I evoke the spirit of my grandmother or the Tshishimbi dance, I enter into this other world.

The performative aspect of my poetry informs the writing, especially when I know that the text will be part of a musical or artistic creation. This was the case with the poem "Virtues," written at the behest of the saxophonist Patrick Dunst, and subsequently declaimed or sung with his musical ensemble. My long poem "The Slaughterhouse of Dreams or the First Human, Bende's Folly" also got its start in this way. The Congolese visual artist Sammy Baloji had invited me to contribute a poetic text about the Congo. Accepting his invitation, I was inspired by the way that the kasala is built around specific themes and variations. The kasala form is structured around a "backbone," from which the singer diverges when they improvise. The performance of this clan song hinges on the singer's ability to draw forth memories and reinvent them. I produced a first draft with several themes and possibilities for structural variation. Next, I went into the studio with Patrick Dunst (saxophone, bass clarinet) and Grilli Pollheimer (percussion). We spent an hour improvising—or rather reinventing—the poems. Finally, I used the recording to put the finishing touches on the kasala. With my musical accompanists, we unveiled the results of our experimentation at the Museum Rietberg as part of an exhibition featuring Baloji. Subsequently, Baloji has created installations based on this performance.

Themes from jazz, soul, and even the blues overlap with those of the kasala. Hence my taste for these styles of music.

Wauters: Do you see connections between your poetry and your novel-writing and playwriting? Or are they totally separate practices?

Mwanza Mujila: Poetry is the transmission belt of everything I write. Whether a short story or a novel, I pile up the same vocabulary, the same rhetorical sallies, and, to a certain extent, the same insolence. I am fundamentally a poet. I refuse to cut the umbilical cord when I put on my novelist's or playwright's coat. In my eyes—this is a personal opinion, and therefore a subjective, potentially idiosyncratic one—poetry is the mother, sister, and grandmother of literature.

I should add that writing in a language different from the one you speak in daily life leaves traces in your work. I experience more and more gaps in memory when I write in French. The mechanics—the spontaneity, the inner music of the language, the arrangement of the words—grows rusty. In response, I have created a personal dictionary and stylistic approach to call upon when in need. I scribble words in school notebooks that I leaf through before writing a first draft, as well as during rewrites. I rough out poems in French for the sole purpose of keeping the French language warm. Later, I make use of these texts in my novels and plays.

Wauters: Since the success of *Tram 83*, which was translated into multiple languages, your books have traveled the world. I can't help but find this beautiful, because it seems to me that it's a theme that links all your works: the desire to build bridges between continents, to reunite what was divided. How do you experience this great journey of your work?

Mwanza Mujila: Writing is a surprising activity. You create (out of whole cloth) characters. You feed them as one does with plants or animals—with sun, with water, with hay. You give them a body, a soul, an identity, desires, extravagances. You keep them on a leash from morning till night. They breathe by your will alone. You can defenestrate them from your manuscript, make them wretched, hideous, or even perish. But just as soon as the book is published, the characters skedaddle. They go join the rebellion. Now they belong to the community of readers. The gap widens further when the book is translated and the characters express themselves in languages that the writer does not speak. Each time my texts appear in an unknown language,

I experience satisfaction accompanied by a feeling of regret. It is something on the order of *saudade*. But for my characters, it's paradise. A Danish reader of *Tram 83* or a South African reader of my poetry discovers my books according to the lights of their own culture and past readings. In this way the protagonists of my books begin a dialogue with literary figures from other linguistic universes. This is the miracle of literature, the possibility of a world without borders.

Maney: Thinking about the global reach of your writing, and how translation inevitably alters its reception in different cultural spaces, I feel like these poems have so much to say to Anglophone readers in 2025 about global ecology and the so-called Green Revolution. Not everyone knows that the Democratic Republic of Congo is by far the world's largest supplier of cobalt as well as a leading producer of other metals crucial to building the lithium-ion batteries and new technologies billed as our last hope to avert a climate apocalypse. Yet your poems show how this vision for a green future merely transfers untold human suffering and environmental destruction out of view of the West to the Congo, and, more broadly, the Global South. We witness children digging cobalt underground without safety equipment or schlepping heavy loads of ore for miles, waterways polluted with chemicals, decimated landscapes. Is it fair to say that *The Slaughterhouse of Dreams* gives the lie to these Western discourses of sustainability and green revolution? Are they, to quote from one of your kasala, yet another bitter "farce that dare not speak its name"?

Mwanza Mujila: I don't go in for invective or denunciation of this or that Western company. That said, it wouldn't be wrong to assert that certain Western discourses regarding Africa and Africans amount to little more than a sham—that is to say, propaganda and demagoguery. They do not reflect the reality on the ground or even the aspirations of the people who are primarily concerned by them.

In the Katanga where I was born and raised, everything revolves around minerals. Had my family not enjoyed a comfortable social standing, I might already have died in a mining accident, I might be digging in a mine as we speak. I know people who have died in cave-ins. I know people, mothers and fathers, who have lost their children in the mines. I know people who have died of alcoholism (as a rule, miners use alcohol to brace themselves up). I know people who are still laboring in the mines. I speak about these people, not in an anodyne way or from the sidelines, but with the sensitivity and authenticity of an eyewitness. I observe, I see things, and I write what I see.

As I often say, the Congo is a postcolonial colony. It was imagined originally as a territory for the extraction of wealth. Yesterday, it was ivory, rubber, and minerals. Today, it is still minerals. To put an end to the brutal exploitation of humans and nature, the Congolese authorities must assume responsibility, and there must be, in addition, international solidarity. The truth? We are still light years away from that. Tomorrow and the day after tomorrow, children will continue to toil in the mines.

Wauters: You live today in Austria. Would you write the same books if you resided elsewhere, in the Congo, for example? I ask you this because it's my belief that we write from loss, from the standpoint of what we miss most dearly. Your literary terrain seems to be constituted by the wound inflicted on your country. That's where your books start, it's the point to which they return. Do you agree with this observation?

Mwanza Mujila: Completely. In my case, the loss is double, without even adding that I was born in Zaire, a country that no longer exists. The loss—or rip or tear, because any loss is one—of the national space is augmented by the scission of the linguistic environment in which I was born and grew up, in which I first fell in love, in which I learned to read and write. I live in Austria, I no longer speak French on a daily basis, but I write in this language. I landed in Europe as an adult. All my literary culture was acquired in French—the administrative language of the Congo—and secondarily in Lingala and Swahili. For a writer—let's call them an eccentric who trades in language and words—this deprivation (even if willed) carries weight. I feel like I don't have a language or that I've been reborn multiple times within a single lifetime.

Residing in a foreign country is an uncanny experience. I realize this anew whenever I travel to Lubumbashi, my hometown. I have become a stranger there, a revenant, a hybrid, even if no one says it to my face. I am no longer entitled to the same secrets, the same confidences of yesteryear. When I land, it's an open secret that I am only passing through, that tomorrow, or the day after, I will return by the same route. The reality of no longer sharing the same daily life, of not attending weddings or second marriages, of not showing up at funerals and burials, of not having to endure the same floods, the same brazen elections, the same shortages of running water and electricity, of not being with people during their illnesses and accomplishments, puts you on the sidelines in more than one sense. What's more, your marginality is plain to all: you no longer master the subtleties of local languages, the meanings of jokes escape you, you're unable to do the new dance . . . There is no such thing as happy exile. That being said, every departure is a choice. It is not necessarily connected to the curse—*tshishotu*. I accept my fate.

I would not have written the same books if I had continued living in the Congo. I might have become a bartender, a musician, a French teacher, a mining official or trader somewhere in Katanga. All of the fellow writers whom I grew up with have thrown in the towel.

Living in the West triggers an unusual relationship with one's native country; I see it differently, I understand it better. The Congo drags behind it more than a century of astounding violence: colonization, secessions, a repetition of wars, dictatorships. I needed spatial and linguistic separation to uncover hidden meanings and reinvent the nation. In my work, the Congo is above all a fictional construct, or rather a country of fantasy, apprehended from the perspective of the margins and loss.

The place where you write from changes the art you make. My first literary genealogy included French, Francophone, and African writers: Rimbaud, Mudimbe, Hugo, Camus, Breton . . . In Lubumbashi, my city of birth, these were the authors I could get my hands on most easily without having to sell my soul to the devil. My second literary genealogy was linked to writers from the Americas, English-speaking Africa, and a few Europeans like Dostoyevsky. My current genealogy is made up of Germanophone writers and poets as well as those from Eastern Europe. As soon as I unpacked my bags in Germany, and then in Graz, I began to study German and discover names like Kleist, Bernhard, Pilinszky, Kosovel, Mayröcher, and Bachmann. While all these writers do not surface in my writing, I nonetheless give them credit for having lighted my way.

Wauters: Your books make your readers want to dance, did you know that? The rumba, the cha-cha-cha. It's as if you wrote to take revenge on the sadness and ugliness that envelop us. To give birth to stars that dance. Is there some of that in your work? As in Nietzsche, an obstinate search for joy?

Mwanza Mujila: I don't write to move mountains, to turn water into palm wine, or even to bring about social change. I don't set myself goals of that sort as a writer. I'm a longtime music lover and come from a country where music is part of the celebration of daily life. Music permeates my work without asking my permission to enter. Music gives rise to an essentially joyous world of sound. This is obviously to the profit of my characters, the poet I am, and my potential readers.

Every work is a musical composition. Writing presupposes the arrangement of language, and thus, of sounds and images. You join them, string them together, pile them up . . . In my case, I try to use the French language like Max Roach used his drums, Masekela his trumpet, Dudu Pukwana his saxophone, Bheki Mseleku his piano. A language has a body, even if there is no blood running through it. When I give birth to my poems, I feel the language passing through my fingers like a sheet, an animal, an ore. The poet's job is to change that copper ore or that snake into something imaginative, full of delight.

Let's come back to music: it's the tip of the iceberg. As a writer, I try, using the prehistoric means at my disposal, to bring humanity down from its pedestal. Music is perhaps just one way, one kind of lifeline, to purge us of our bad luck.

Translator's Acknowledgments

There are a number of people whose work and kindness informed the making of this translation. I would like to thank our editor, Shook; the visual artist Sammy Baloji, for permitting us to reproduce several of his photographs of Katangese mining pits in this volume; our U.S. publisher, Will Evans, and his crack team at Deep Vellum; David Giannoni and Antoine Wauters at L'Arbre à Paroles, with a special nod to Wauters for allowing me to translate and adapt his interview with Mwanza Mujila; and Mark Welzel and the curators and organizers of the 2019 *Fiktion Kongo* exhibition at the Museum Rietberg in Zürich, who originally commissioned the translation of many of the kasala that appear in this book.

Additional support for this translation was provided by a PSC-CUNY Award, jointly funded by The Professional Staff Congress and The City University of New York. The translation also benefited from exchanges I had with graduate students while teaching in the Literary Translation program at the CUNY Graduate Center.

Finally, the author and translator wish to thank the editors of the following journals, in which certain translations first appeared: *Asymptote* ("Kasala for Myself 1"), *Poetry International* ("Kasala for Myself 2," "Kasala for My Kaku 1," "Kasala for My Kaku 2"), and *lyrikline* ("The City Within").

Biographical Information

FISTON MWANZA MUJILA was born in the Democratic Republic of Congo in 1981 and lives today in Austria. His debut novel, *Tram 83*, published in English in 2015 by Deep Vellum, won the Etisalat Prize for Literature and the German International Literature Award and was longlisted for both the International Booker Prize and the Prix littéraire du Monde. His second novel, *The Villain's Dance* (2024), also available from Deep Vellum, won the Prix Les Afriques and was a finalist for the National Book Award for Translated Literature. In addition to these novels translated by Roland Glasser, his poetry collection *The River in the Belly* (trans. J. Bret Maney, 2021) is also available in English from Deep Vellum. Dubbed "a new and provocative contribution to African Literature," it was a finalist for the Luschei Prize for African Poetry and the Sarah Maguire Prize for Poetry in Translation.

J. BRET MANEY is a literary critic and translator from the French and Spanish. He is a recipient of several awards, including the 2020 Gulf Coast Translation Prize for his translations of Fiston Mwanza Mujila's poetry and an International Latino Book Award and PEN/Heim Translation Fund Grant for his translation of Guillermo Cotto-Thorner's novel, *Manhattan Tropics* (Arte Público, 2019), which he also coedited. He is Associate Professor of English and Digital Humanities at Lehman College and The Graduate Center, CUNY.

SAMMY BALOJI (b. 1978) lives and works between Lubumbashi and Brussels. His visual art explores the cultural, architectural, and industrial heritage of the Katanga region and critiques the impact of Belgian colonization. A Chevalier des Arts et des Lettres, he has received numerous fellowships, awards, and distinctions—including at the African Photography Encounters of Bamako and the Dakar Biennale. In 2019–2020, he was a resident of the French Academy in Rome–Villa Medici. Recent solo exhibitions include *The King's Order to Dance*, Galerie Imane Farès, Paris (2023) and *K(C)ongo, Fragments of Interlaced Dialogues*, Palazzo Pitti, Florence (2022) and Beaux-Arts de Paris (2021). He has participated in the 35th Bienal de São Paulo (2023), the Architecture Biennale of Venice (2023), the 15th Sharjah Biennial (2023), and the Sydney Biennale (2020).

ANTOINE WAUTERS, born in Liège in 1981, is a Belgian poet and novelist. He is the author of *Nos mères* (Prix Révélation SGDL, Prix Première), *Pense aux pierres sous tes pas, Mahmoud ou la montée des eaux* (Prix Wepler, Prix Marguerite Duras, Prix du Livre Inter, and translated into more than a dozen languages), all published by Éditions Verdier, and *Le Musée des contradictions* (Éditions du sous-sol), winner of the 2022 Prix Goncourt de la Nouvelle. At L'Arbre à paroles, where Wauters is director of the "iF" book series, he has edited three volumes of Fiston Mwanza Mujila's poetry.

www.ingramcontent.com/pod-product-compliance
Lightning Source LLC
Jackson TN
JSHW082357051025
91572JS00001B/1
* 9 7 8 1 6 4 6 0 5 4 1 1 4 *